Library o f Congress Number TXu 2-225-374
ISBN 9780578800103

Front Cover design by Artist, Maria C. Friscia
Photographs and Book Design by Christine M. Lemons

About the Author

Christine M. Lemons is a retired
elementary school teacher
with interests in Photography, Nature, and the Arts.

"During the covid-19 pandemic,
a robin's nest appeared
at my home in Michigan.
I photographed the birds
making their nest,
laying eggs, hatching babies,
feeding them, their growth,
and finally their
departure
flight."

This book is dedicated to my awesome grandchildren,
and all the wonderful children I've had the privilege to teach and learn with!

***

Special appreciation and thankfulness to my husband, Don,
for his help with setting up the camera,
to my friends, for their uplifting encouragement,
and to God, for the beauty of Nature.

Hmmm...
Dead grass is o[n]
top of my dec[k]
light!

And, it keeps
coming back
after I take
it off!

I wonder how [it]
got there!

Look! There's a Mama Robin on the deck!

She's building a nest!

First she puts sticks and dry grass.

Then she adds dirt and mud.

Last, she adds more dry grass.

1

Several days later,
there's one blue egg in the nest!

2

3

4

Every few days, I see one more egg!

Mama and Papa Robin protect the nest and keep it clean inside!

There's four pretty blue eggs
in the nest!

After several more days, two eggs hatch! The babies are mini, pink fluffs!

A few days later, another one hatches! Now, there's three babies and one egg!

Finally, the last one hatches!
Four small, furry baby robins
are in the nest!

Can you see their beaks

My friend helps me name them: "Eeny, Meeny, Miny and Mo!"

Mama and Papa Robin hunt for food all day long to feed them.

Their orange beaks open wide. They are hungry babies!

They chirp loudly and always want for more food.

They eat, and eat, and eat and EAT!
(Do you see Mama's belly?)

They eat a lot
of insects.

Worms are
their favorite!

Eeny, Meeny,
Miny and Mo
expand,
and grow
super
FAST!

Their wings sprou
and spread out!

They grow, and grow, and grow and GROW!

There is not much space in the nest now. It is FULL!

They flap,
and extend
their wings.

They watch how
Mama and Papa fly
out to look for food
in the forest.

I imagine they
will soon try to
fly high,
up into the sky!

I believe we will soon have to say,
"Goodbye! Adios! Ciao!"

Look!
They are getting ready
to leave!

First, goes Eeny!

Then, follows Meeny!

Next, flies Miny!

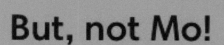

But, not Mo!

Oh no!

Mo is afraid to go!

The next day,
Mama nudges Mo.
She tweets, "It's okay, Mo
Be brave! It is time to Go

Finally, Mo takes the leap.
His wings flutter bravely.
"Good-bye Mo!"

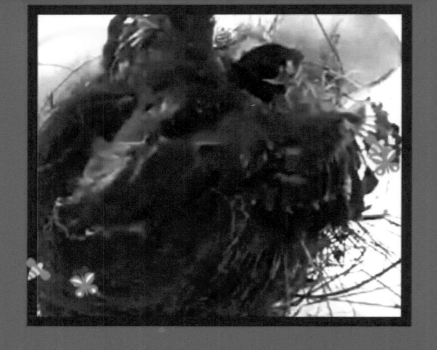

I sing,
   "Have fun,
      Eeny,
         Meeny,
            Miny...
               and Mo!"

I wonder where they will go.
I wonder if they will come back.

What do you think?

QUESTIONS

1. What do you like about this story? What don't you like?

2. How many insects, bugs, and worms can you find?   Which one do you like the best
Why?

3. How many are bees? How many are butterflies? How many are ladybugs?

4. Are their more bees or worms? Are there more butterflies or dragonflies?
Are more ladybugs or spiders?

5. Do you think Eeny, Meeny, Miny and Mo are still together? Do you think they will co
back?

6. Draw a picture of where they went. Are they in another state or country? Are they
together?

7. Write a story about where they went. What did they see? What did they do?.

8. Write a story about them coming back. What season is it? Do you think they'll build
new nest? Where?

CPSIA information can be obtained
at www.ICGtesting.com
Printed in the USA
BVHW051330230221
600892BV00012B/171

* 9 7 8 0 5 7 8 8 0 0 1 0 3 *